TOOLS FOR CAREGIVERS

- **ATOS:** 0.5
- **GRL:** C
- **WORD COUNT:** 29

- **CURRICULUM CONNECTIONS:** animals, insects, nature

Skills to Teach

- **HIGH-FREQUENCY WORDS:** a, go, I, in, is, it, let, put, see, them
- **CONTENT WORDS:** catch, dark, fireflies, glow, jar, watch
- **PUNCTUATION:** exclamation point, periods
- **WORD STUDY:** long /e/, spelled ee (*see*); long /i/, spelled *ie* (*fireflies*); long /o/, spelled *ow* (*glow*); compound word (*fireflies*); multisyllable word (*fireflies*)
- **TEXT TYPE:** information report

Before Reading Activities

- Read the title and give a simple statement of the main idea.
- Have students "walk" though the book and talk about what they see in the pictures.
- Introduce new vocabulary by having students predict the first letter and locate the word in the text.
- Discuss any unfamiliar concepts that are in the text.

After Reading Activities

Fireflies are very unique. They can produce light! Ask the readers if they can name any other animals that light up. What are some other unique traits that insects or animals have? List their examples on the board. If the unique trait is an action or sound, can the readers act or sound them out?

Tadpole Books are published by Jump!, 5357 Penn Avenue South, Minneapolis, MN 55419, www.jumplibrary.com

Copyright ©2019 Jump. International copyright reserved in all countries. No part of this book may be reproduced in any form without written permission from the publisher.

Editor: Jenna Trnka **Designer:** Michelle Sonnek

Photo Credits: khlungcenter/Shutterstock, cover; Holly Looney/Imagemore/SuperStock, 1; Klagyivik Viktor/Shutterstock, 2–3, 16tm; Simon Shim/Shutterstock, 4–5, 16tr; Fer Gregory/Shutterstock, 6–7, 10–11, 16bl, 16bm; terekhov igor/Shutterstock, 8–9 (net), 16tl; IamTK/Shutterstock, 8–9 (firefly), 16tl; Suzanne Tucker/Shutterstock, 12–13, 16br; Phil Degginger/Age Fotostock, 14–15.

Library of Congress Cataloging-in-Publication Data
Names: Nilsen, Genevieve, author.
Title: I see fireflies / by Genevieve Nilsen.
Description: Minneapolis, MN: Jump!, Inc., (2019) | Series: Backyard bugs | Includes index.
Identifiers: LCCN 2018016035 (print) | LCCN 2018017340 (ebook) | ISBN 9781641282307 (ebook) | ISBN 9781641282284 (hardcover: alk. paper) | ISBN 9781641282291 (paperback)
Subjects: LCSH: Fireflies—Juvenile literature.
Classification: LCC QL596.L28 (ebook) | LCC QL596.L28 N55 2018 (print) | DDC 595.76/44—dc23
LC record available at https://lccn.loc.gov/2018016035

I SEE FIREFLIES

by Genevieve Nilsen

TABLE OF CONTENTS

tadpole
books

I SEE FIREFLIES

It is dark.

firefly

I see fireflies.

I see them glow!

7

I catch them.

jar

I put them in a jar.

I watch them.

I let them go.

WORDS TO KNOW

catch

dark

fireflies

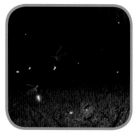

glow

jar

watch

INDEX